Dynasties of China

Reader

Core Knowledge®

ISBN: 978-1-68380-145-0

Dynasties of China

Table of Contents

Dynasties of China
Reader
Core Knowledge History and Geography™

Chapter 1
The First Emperor

The Emperor's Clay Army In the spring of 1974, some villagers in central China needed a new well. The well diggers' muscles ached as they dug deeper and deeper into the reddish soil, looking for water. At twelve feet down they hit something—but not water.

It was a head! Not a human head, but a life-sized head made of terracotta, or clay. The face startled them because it looked so real, but it clearly came from an earlier time. The workers kept digging and they eventually uncovered the complete figure of a Chinese warrior buried for more than two thousand years.

Archaeologists rushed to the site of the well. They carefully dug up the whole area. They found more clay soldiers, then still more, and clay horses, too. In all, they found a whole army of life-sized soldiers and horses—about seven thousand of them!

The Big Question

What were some of the things the first emperor did to unite China?

Vocabulary

terracotta, n. baked or hardened brownish-red clay

emperor, n. the ruler of an empire

jade, n. a hard mineral, usually green, that can be made into jewelry or small figurines

These life-sized soldiers were part of the vast clay army that guarded the entrance to the tomb of China's first emperor. Chinese emperors believed that they would enter an afterlife that would be like their life on Earth. So they buried their most valuable possessions with them—precious silks, priceless objects of jade or bronze, and musical instruments.

Each warrior had his own personality. Some seemed angry, while others appeared cheerful. The soldiers wore armor made of clay. They carried real weapons—bows and arrows, swords, spears, and **crossbows**.

Guardians of the Tomb

The clay army stood in silent formation, guarding the tomb of the first emperor of China. Alert and ready for battle, they were to protect the emperor from evil spirits and robbers. If a robber did manage to break in, he might not escape in one piece—the clay army surrounded the tomb.

Over seven hundred thousand workers built the first emperor's tomb and created his army of clay. And it took them almost

 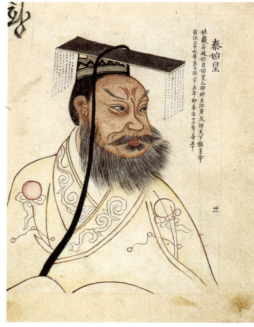

Figures such as this archer were part of the army created for the tomb of Shihuangdi, China's first emperor. Shihuangdi ruled from 221–210 BCE.

forty years to do it. The emperor did not want anyone to know about the tomb and its contents. So after he died, many workers in the underground tomb found that they could not get out. Walls and doors sealed them inside the tomb forever. They were buried alive to keep the emperor's secret.

Uniting the Country

The first emperor frightened everyone. Named Zheng (/jung/) at birth, the emperor came from the northwest Chinese state of Qin (/chin/).

When Zheng was a young boy, China was not a single unified country as it is today. Instead, many separate states existed, and they fought one another. Zheng became king of the state of Qin when he was thirteen—probably not too much older than you are now. To keep his power, he had to fight wars with his neighbors. After ruling as king for twenty-five years, he defeated all the other states.

In 221 BCE Zheng declared himself emperor of all of China and took the name Shihuangdi (/shur*hwong*dee/), meaning First Supreme Emperor. Shihuangdi established the Qin dynasty, named after his home state.

Shihuangdi had to be very tough to hold the new country together. His old enemies still hated him, so he commanded that all the weapons in the empire be brought to the capital city. He melted the weapons down and turned them into harmless bells and twelve enormous statues that he placed inside his palace.

Shihuangdi struggled to unite the many different states into one nation. Each of the old states had its own particular kind of writing, calendar, and system of weights and measures. This caused great confusion. How could you understand a written command from the emperor if you did not use the same kind of writing as he did? Even the money was different all over China. Some places used coins in the shape of knives, while others used coins shaped like shovels or fish or small scallop shells. Which one was the most valuable? And if you and your neighbors measured out grain differently, who decided which was the right amount?

Shihuangdi decided to remove these differences. He insisted that all people use the same written language so that everyone in the empire could understand each other. Shihuangdi declared that all coins must be round with a square hole in the middle.

Here you can see different kinds of money used before Emperor Shihuangdi made everyone use the same round coins.

This was done so that coins could be strung together. The emperor established one calendar and one single system of weighing and measuring goods that everyone had to follow.

Shihuangdi wanted to travel easily throughout his empire, so he ordered the building of canals to connect the great waterways of China. He also commanded that roads be built—four thousand miles of them! Trees lining the roads provided shade for travelers.

A Cruel Ruler

Such improvements made life easier for the Chinese people. But the emperor could also be very cruel. He hated crime, and people who broke his laws were punished in horrible ways.

Shihuangdi hated any ideas that were different from his own, and he hated it when scholars looked back on the past and said life was better back then. He had every book of history, philosophy, and literature in all of China collected and burned. He commanded that four hundred monks be killed because they made a promise to him that they could not keep. Even the emperor's own son was upset, and he told his father it was wrong to be so cruel. But you shouldn't talk back to your parents—especially if the parent is a **tyrant**! Shihuangdi became angry at his son and sent him far away, all the way to the northern edge of China.

> **Vocabulary**
>
> **tyrant,** n. a leader who rules by cruel or unjust means

The Wall Builder

Shihuangdi gave his son a job to keep him busy. He told him to supervise the construction of a series of walls in northern China.

Some old walls were already standing. Shihuangdi wanted to connect some of these walls and build new ones. The wall building did not end with Shihuangdi. Later dynasties built more walls. The rulers of the **Ming dynasty** built the last and most

Vocabulary

Ming dynasty, n. a period of Chinese rule from the late 1300s to the mid-1600s

elaborate ones. These Ming-dynasty walls are the ones that we usually think of as the Great Wall of China. But the work began many years earlier, and the Chinese honor Shihuangdi as the first great wall builder.

Construction of the Great Wall of China began under the rule of Shihuangdi.

8

The Great Wall snakes through China's mountains and deserts for more than one thousand miles. Why in the world would anyone need such gigantic walls? Shihuangdi ordered the walls to be built to keep out the people who lived beyond the northern border of China.

The Europeans called these northern people the Huns; the Chinese called them the Xiongnu (/syoong*noo/). The Xiongnu were nomads, which means they had no permanent homes and moved from place to place. They moved around on their great herds of horses, riding like the wind. They wandered the open grasslands, called steppes (/steps/), in search of good grass for their horses to eat. When they found a place where they wanted to stay briefly, they would set up large tent-like houses called yurts that they could take down quickly when they were ready to move.

In contrast, the Chinese at that time led settled lives. Most of them were farmers who lived in the fertile valleys of the Huang He (/whang/huh/), or Yellow River, in the north and the Yangzi (/yang*see/) River

> **Vocabulary**
>
> **barbarian,** n. a violent or uncivilized person

farther south. They rarely left their farms and villages. To the settled Chinese, the nomadic Xiongnu seemed like **barbarians**.

The Xiongnu were fierce warriors. They would mount their swift horses and swoop down on Chinese villages, raiding and stealing from the people who lived there. Shihuangdi was determined to protect China from these northern raiders, and so he started building walls.

He sent three hundred thousand soldiers and workers—including criminals who had to march hundreds of miles in chains—to the northern border. Many died on the way. Once they got there, there was no food. Half-starved, the men had to work anyway.

Searching for Immortality

In his later years the emperor became worried about dying. Shihuangdi was determined to find a magic potion that would help him live forever. He sent out several sea expeditions in search of islands that were supposed to hold the secret to **immortality**. Of course, the expeditions failed.

Vocabulary

immortality, n.
unending life

In his capital city, Shihuangdi set about building several palaces and gardens for himself. The emperor became so fearful that he slept in a different palace every night. He moved secretly, and no one except his closest advisers knew where he was.

Shihuangdi was a mysterious figure during his lifetime—and even his death remained a secret. The emperor died while on his way home from a long trip. Only a few advisers knew about it, and they did not want anyone else to find out. The only problem was that the emperor's decaying body was beginning to smell! How could they hide that? They came up with a plan to have a cart full of rotten fish follow the emperor's carriage until they got back to the capital. That way people would think it was the fish that stank, and not the recently deceased emperor!

Shihuangdi had boasted that his descendants would rule for ten thousand **generations**. But within just a few years of his death, the Qin dynasty collapsed. Another emperor emerged, and another ruling family took over China and founded a new dynasty.

> **Vocabulary**
>
> **generation,** n. a period of time of about twenty-five years

Chapter 2
The Han Dynasty

The Emperor with Seventy-two Spots What sort of person do you think would be the founder of a new dynasty? Someone from a rich and powerful family? Not necessarily. The emperor Liu Bang (/lee*oh/bahng/) was a poor, uneducated peasant.

The Big Question

Why might the Chinese have wanted to protect their silk industry?

Even as a young man, Liu Bang was unusual. His left thigh had seventy-two spots on it, and it was said that a woman once saw a dragon over his head while he slept. According to the Chinese, these things indicated that he would achieve greatness one day.

A powerful warrior, Liu Bang took control of all of China and declared himself the emperor of the Han (/hahn/) dynasty. This dynasty would last for four hundred years.

漢高祖

Liu Bang founded the Han dynasty, which ruled for four hundred years.

Liu Bang lived in a grand palace in the capital city of Chang'an (/chahng*ahn/). The emperor wanted his father to come live with him. "Forget your old farm," he told his father. "Come live here like the richest man on Earth, in the most luxurious palace in all of China."

But his father wasn't sure. He thought he would miss his old home and small village too much. Have you ever had to move? Maybe you felt sad leaving your old home. Well, Liu Bang's father felt the same way.

But Liu Bang was determined to get his father to move, so he had an exact copy of his father's village created near the capital. He moved his father's friends to the new place. He even moved the cows and chickens from the old village so that his father would feel right at home. Only then did Liu Bang's father move.

But all was not peaceful in China. Shihuangdi's walls had not stopped the Xiongnu. They continued to pour over the walls and into China. Liu Bang and the emperors who came after him made war against the northern horsemen, but still the raiders came. What could the Chinese do about them?

A later Han emperor, Wudi (/woo*dee/), had an idea. Maybe other states would be willing to fight the hated Xiongnu. But the Chinese didn't know anything about other lands or other peoples.

China had always been isolated from the rest of the world because of its geography. The Pacific Ocean lay to the east of China; to the west lay the Himalayas, with some of the tallest mountains in the world; to the north were vast steppes and the forbidding Gobi (/go*bee/) Desert; and to the south lay more mountains and jungles.

Because the Chinese were so isolated, they believed they were the center of the world. They called their country the Middle Kingdom or All Under Heaven. They had little interest in exploring other places.

One day in 138 BCE, Emperor Wudi ordered a court official by the name of Zhang Qian to go out into the wilderness. Wudi commanded this **official** to find another

Vocabulary

official, n. a person who carries out a government duty

The Geography of China

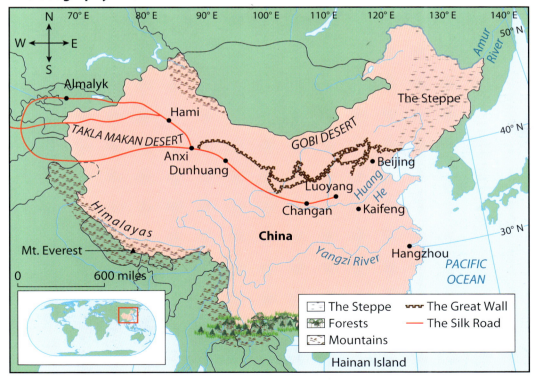

China's geography varies greatly and kept it isolated from the rest of the world.

state that would help China fight the northern **tribesmen**. The explorer headed west into central Asia. He discovered amazing things, including the most wonderful horses he'd ever seen.

Zhang Qian went as far as the state of Bactria (/back*tree*yuh/), which is now called Afghanistan (/af*gan*ih*stan/). He asked the people of Bactria to help the Chinese fight the Xiongnu. But they said no.

Disappointed, Zhang Qian returned to China. He probably thought he had failed in his mission. But his stories about the western land fascinated the Chinese. People in China listened carefully when they heard about the magnificent horses in Central Asia. In particular,

The Akhal-Teke horse, or Heavenly Horse, also known as the "sweats blood horse," was a prized possession in China. It was one of the first horses to be brought to China from Central Asia.

they became interested in a horse known as a "sweats blood horse." This horse was viewed as special and exotic.

The Silk Road

As well as horses, the Chinese loved silk. Silk was a precious, valuable fabric. Have you ever felt silk? It is very soft and beautiful. The Chinese got silk by raising special worms, called silkworms. They'd feed the silkworms mulberry leaves. In the springtime the worms would spin a cocoon made of delicate threads. The Chinese learned how to unwind those threads and weave them into a beautiful fabric.

At that time, the Chinese were the only ones in the world who knew how to make silk, and they wanted to keep it that way. Silkworm eggs were not allowed out of the country. If you tried to sneak them out, you would be punished with death.

Silk has been made and highly valued in China for more than six thousand years. These illustrations show silk being woven. After the thread has been dyed, it is then dried.

But finished Chinese silk could leave the country, and when foreigners saw the fabric they immediately wanted to trade for it. The silk trade created wealth for China.

That was how the Silk Road began. The road was really a system of trails that stretched thousands of miles across the mountains and deserts of Central Asia. Traders traveled in groups called caravans. Animals such as camels and **yaks** carried the silk. The route led from one **oasis** to the next. The caravan would stop at each oasis to rest in the shade and get food and water before continuing on in the desert. Following this route, silk traders made it all the way to the countries on the Mediterranean Sea.

> **Vocabulary**
>
> **yak,** n. an ox-like animal that lives in Asia
>
> **oasis,** n. an area in the desert where there are water and plants

People of the Mediterranean world were eager to buy China's silk. Cleopatra, the queen of Egypt, wore a silk gown to impress her guests. Silk was so popular in Rome that the emperor had to forbid men from wearing it so that there would be enough for the women.

Making Paper

The Han dynasty, founded by Liu Bang, lasted from 206 BCE to 220 CE, roughly the same period as the mighty Roman Empire. But in many ways the Han culture was far more advanced than that of Rome. The Chinese themselves look upon this dynasty as a kind of golden time. They still call themselves the sons of Han.

One of the great achievements of the Han dynasty was the invention of paper. The Chinese made paper by mashing together a variety of ingredients including tree bark, **hemp**, rags, and fish nets.

Can you imagine not having any paper? What would you write on? Before paper was invented, the Chinese used the bones of animals, strips of bamboo, or even precious silk.

The invention of paper was a huge advance. It would be another one thousand years before paper would appear in Europe.

Chapter 3
Wu Zhao

City of Foreigners In the year 638 CE, an imperial carriage hurried through the countryside on its way to Chang'an, the capital city of China. The carriage rocked and swayed as it went. In the back of the carriage sat a thirteen-year-old girl named Wu Zhao (/woo/jow/).

The Big Question

Why might it be said that Wu Zhao's rise to power was an extraordinary achievement?

The young girl was going to live in the **imperial** palace. The emperor at that time was Taizong (/tye*dzoong/) of the Tang dynasty.

Can you imagine how Wu Zhao must have felt? She had probably never been away from her home and her family before. However, Wu's mother had become a widow and had decided that her daughter would be better off living in the palace.

Vocabulary

foreigner, n. a person who comes from another country

imperial, adj. relating to an emperor, empress or empire

唐武后　武則天

Wu Zhao became the only woman to ever rule China as an empress.

Wu Zhao's New Life

In the back of the carriage, young Wu Zhao must have been excited and scared about her new life. The roads became crowded as they approached the city of Chang'an, the largest and grandest city in the entire world at that time. Merchants carrying luxury goods from the Silk Road filled the streets leading to the capital. The carriage came to a high wall. It prepared to pass through one of the four great gates that led into the city.

Wu Zhao saw amazing things. Roughly one million people lived in Chang'an. Many of them were foreigners—Koreans, Japanese, Arabs, Persians, Turks, Indians, and even Africans. Wu Zhao had never seen so many different kinds of people. They looked strange to her. They spoke languages she could not understand. Everyone on the streets, even the Chinese themselves, dressed like foreigners. Women wore tightly fitted dresses that followed the fashions of Persia. Rich Chinese men wore hats made of leopard skin. The music that rose up in the streets was unlike anything she had ever heard. In the two great city marketplaces, merchants sold exotic goods—foods, plants, perfumes, medicines, fabrics, and jewels from foreign lands.

As her carriage drove through the streets, Wu Zhao saw many monasteries, temples, and **shrines** for the **Buddhist religion** that had come to China from India. She saw

> ### Vocabulary
>
> **shrine,** n. a place considered holy because it is associated with a religious person or saint
>
> **Buddhist religion,** n. also called Buddhism, a religion originating in India that is based on the teachings of Siddhartha Gautama

houses topped with yellow roofs that were curved to guard against evil spirits, which were believed to move only in straight paths.

The Imperial City

Wu Zhao's carriage went up the Street of the Red Bird, a very wide street that stretched 480 feet from one side to the other. At the end of the street lay the walled Imperial City. The emperor lived and worked within these walls, and only certain people could enter this special city within a city. All others were forbidden to do so. Even touching the wall was a serious crime. If you dared to put your hand on the wall, you could be hit seventy times with a rod.

The guards at the wall allowed Wu Zhao's carriage to pass through the gate. They could tell immediately that the carriage belonged to the emperor because it was painted a brilliant red, the same color as the emperor's court.

Inside the official court, seated on his throne, Emperor Taizong issued commands that affected a large portion of Asia. He ruled over a vast empire that included sixty million people. Thousands of government officials scurried about the huge rooms with marble floors, carrying out his orders and meeting his every desire.

But Wu Zhao went to an even more secret part of the Imperial City, the place where Taizong lived. Only the emperor and members of his household could enter what was called the Palace City. The emperor was the only grown man allowed inside the Palace City; even the emperor's sons had to leave when they grew up.

Emperor Taizong is considered the co-founder of the Tang dynasty and one of China's greatest emperors.

Life in the Palace City

The emperor had one wife but many female companions, all of whom lived in the Palace City. Wu Zhao was destined to be a companion. This would be her new home. She had no idea of what to expect.

Wu Zhao spent her days studying music and literature, and learning to write beautifully. She dressed in gorgeous silk robes and precious jewels. She and the other women in the palace arranged and rearranged their hair and applied makeup. At that time fashionable women painted eyebrows on their faces. The eyebrows were drawn in different ways to create different moods. One style was named "Distant Mountains," and another was called "Sorrow Brows." "Sorrow Brows" was Wu Zhao's style.

The emperor's wife and his companions walked in the gardens and played games together, including the exciting game of polo, a popular game on horseback that had recently come to China from Persia. While riding at high speed, polo players had to hit a ball with a long stick or mallet.

This sculpture from Tang China captures the excitement of polo, a game that had been brought from Persia to China.

Though the female companions enjoyed the games and luxuries of the Palace City, their lives were not free of worry. If any one of the women displeased the emperor, she could lose her privileges or even be sent away from the palace forever.

In 649 CE, Emperor Taizong died, and according to tradition, Wu Zhao and the other women in the palace had to shave their heads and move to a Buddhist temple. They would have to live there as **nuns** for the rest of their lives. Wu Zhao did not want to leave the luxury of the palace. She swore she would find some way to return.

Wu Zhao had already caught the attention of Emperor Taizong's son, Gaozong (/gow*dzoong/). A year after Taizong's death, Gaozong, now the new emperor, commanded that Wu Zhao be returned to the palace. When she returned, Wu Zhao grew her hair back and never again left the imperial court.

Wu Zhao Turns Ruthless

Once Wu Zhao returned to the Palace City, she began to better understand how to survive there. Survival for Wu Zhao meant defeating her enemies, and this is what she set out to do. She cleverly got rid of many of the people who did not favor her, including the emperor's wife and his favorite companions. She secretly killed Gaozong's infant daughter and then tricked him into believing that his wife, the empress, had done it. She then became

Gaozong's favorite companion. Later she became his wife and empress of China.

Empress Wu grew very powerful. She even attended government meetings with Gaozong, which a woman had no right to do in China. Many at court feared her, but they could say nothing. The empress sat behind a screen and whispered to the emperor what he should do. An ancient Chinese historian described how she decided everything, even matters of life and death while "the emperor sat with folded hands."

After Gaozong died, one of their sons and then another took over as emperor, but the real power belonged to Empress Wu. Superstitious and nervous about enemies, Empress Wu planted spies everywhere. But the ghosts of her murdered rivals haunted her. In time, she could no longer stand living in the palace in Chang'an, so she moved the capital to a new location.

Empress Wu was all-powerful. She had everything except the official title of emperor. But she wanted that, too. In 690 CE a flock of bright red birds flew through the room that held the emperor's throne. A phoenix, a bird very special to the empress, was also rumored to have flown over the palace. To the empress it was clear: Heaven had sent these birds to show that she should be the official ruler of China. She made her son **resign**. Wu Zhao declared herself the Holy and Divine Emperor, and the founder of a brand-new dynasty. For the next fifteen years, Wu Zhao ruled as emperor—the first and only time a woman would do so in Chinese history.

> **Vocabulary**
>
> **resign,** v. to step down from or leave a job

The Woman Emperor

Emperor Wu had to overcome the fact that she was a woman in what was traditionally a man's world. She worked hard and became a successful emperor. She ran the empire very skillfully. During her rule, China prospered.

Wu Zhao believed very deeply in Buddhism. She had many temples built, and she ordered the creation of enormous rock sculptures. Caves were hollowed out of rock walls; inside, artists carved giant statues of **Buddha** from stone. Some of the largest cave figures rise as high as a fifteen-story building.

Vocabulary

Buddha, n. the name given to Siddhartha Gautama, the founder of Buddhism

Buddhism became increasingly popular around the time of Empress Wu. These images of Buddha were carved into caves in the countryside.

At eighty years of age, Emperor Wu grew weak and sick. Some of her old enemies saw a chance to get rid of her at last. They killed her closest advisers and put Wu Zhao under house arrest. She died later that year, and the Tang dynasty once again took control in China.

Chapter 4
The Tang Dynasty

Before and After Wu Except for the fifteen years when Wu Zhao ruled as emperor, the Tang dynasty ruled China for almost three hundred years, from 618 CE to 907 CE.

The Big Question

What great advances happened during the Tang Dynasty?

During the Tang dynasty, China was the biggest and richest country in the entire world. It conquered other lands, including Korea, Iran, and a large part of Vietnam. The Japanese were so impressed with China and its culture that they copied much of it, even the written language.

Poetry and the Arts

The Tang emperors loved the arts, especially poetry. Twenty-seven-year-old Xuanzong (/soo*ahn*dzoong/) became emperor in 712 CE. He was skilled in music, poetry, and

Vocabulary

calligraphy, n. artistic handwriting

the art of beautiful writing known as **calligraphy** (/kuh*lihg*ruh*fee/). The new emperor surrounded himself with poets, including two of the most famous poets in Chinese history: Li Bai (/lee*bai/) and Du Fu (/doo*foo/).

Between 607 CE and 838 CE, Japan sent nineteen missions to the Tang court. Knowledge and learning was the main goal of each expedition. For example, priests studied Chinese Buddhism. Officials studied Chinese government. Doctors studied Chinese medicine. Painters studied Chinese art.

Tang China's artistic achievements include ceramic figurines such as this one. These figurines were usually decorated with brightly colored glazes. Like the emperor's terracotta army, these figures were often included in tomb burials.

Du Fu was a very serious and hardworking young man who always wanted to be a government official. Li Bai, on the other hand, took life easier. He wrote:

Life in the World is but a big dream;
I will not spoil it by any labor or care.

Li Bai often got himself into trouble by fighting and drinking too much alcohol. Eventually, Li Bai left the emperor's court and became a wanderer. According to legend, he died by falling into a river. The legend says that while crossing a river in a boat, Li Bai saw the moon's reflection in the water and reached for it, trying to hug it. He fell out of the boat and drowned while reaching for the moon.

An Era of Glory

During the Tang dynasty the country was bursting with creative energy. Foreigners were more welcome than ever before, and the mix of cultures and ideas made China an exciting place.

Tea became incredibly popular during the Tang dynasty. Everyone loved to drink it. Tea was grown in China, and the merchants who sold it became extremely rich. There was only one problem. So much money was being used that China was running out of coins. What do you think the Chinese did? Stopped buying things?

Tea made merchants in Tang China very wealthy.

No, that wasn't the answer. Instead the merchants invented a kind of paper money that they called "flying money," perhaps because the money flew so fast from one person to the next. This was the first type of paper money in the world.

A number of other inventions also took hold. At the end of the Tang dynasty, the invention of **woodblock printing** led to the creation of books. A worker would carve words and drawings onto a wooden block, cover the block with ink, then press it onto a piece of paper. Presto—a printed page! One worker could produce a thousand pages a day using this technique. The oldest existing book in the world, the *Diamond Sutra*, is a Buddhist text that was printed in China in 868 CE. Once again the Chinese outpaced the Europeans: hundreds of years would pass before printing was invented in Europe.

An Explosive Discovery

An even more explosive discovery took place in China during the Tang dynasty. For many centuries, Chinese scientists called **alchemists** had tried to create gold and find the secret to living forever. Their experiments eventually led them to mix **charcoal**, **nitrate**, and **saltpeter** together. The results surprised them—the mixture exploded! The Chinese scientists had discovered gunpowder. A warning appears in a Tang chemistry book: beware when mixing these ingredients because the mixture might explode right in your face and burn off your beard.

Under the Tang dynasty the Chinese used the gunpowder not for warfare but for creating spectacular fireworks. It seems fitting that the brilliant Tang dynasty should be remembered for giving to the world the magnificent gift of fireworks.

Under the Tang dynasty, the Chinese used gunpowder not for warfare but for creating fireworks.

Chapter 5
The Peddler's Curse

The Pancake Prophecy One day in the year 1125, a very strange thing happened to Emperor Hui Zong (/hway/dzoong/) of the Song (/soong/) dynasty. He came upon a poor fish **peddler** sitting in a doorway, eating a pancake.

The Big Question

How did Emperor Hui Zong fall from power?

The peddler offered to share his humble food with the emperor. "Have a bite!" the peddler said to Hui Zong. But Hui Zong was disgusted by the very idea that he, the great emperor, would share a bite of such miserable food. He would not touch it.

Vocabulary

prophecy, n. a prediction about the future

peddler, n. a person who travels from one place to another selling goods

Hui Zong's refusal hurt the peddler's feelings, and the peddler spoke a frightening prophecy. "A day will come," he said to Hui Zong, "when you will be glad to have even a pancake like this."

The emperor went on his way. But the fish peddler's words hung over him like a mysterious curse. Hui Zong was rich and powerful beyond imagination. How could he be happy with just a pancake for a meal? What a ridiculous idea!

In this silk painting, Emperor Hui Zong is shown drinking from a cup made of precious stone.

Hui Zong decided to forget all about his meeting with the peddler. He called for his paints, his brushes, and some paper. Of all the Chinese emperors, Hui Zong stood out as the one who loved art the most. Hui Zong filled his palace with beautiful works of art. He collected six thousand paintings. He learned to paint and write poetry himself. Whenever the business of governing got too boring or too tiring, he sent his officials away so that he could paint a picture or write a poem. He developed new ways to paint birds and flowers, and new styles of calligraphy. He set up an **academy** of painting, and artists from all over the country flocked to it.

"Mountain-Water" Painting

The painters during the Song dynasty (960–1279) did not use oil paints, and they did not work on **canvas**. Instead, these artists used water-based paints on paper and silk. Paint spreads rapidly on those surfaces, so the brush strokes had to be done very quickly and lightly. There could be no hesitation whatsoever.

To the Chinese, paintings of nature were the highest form of art. The artists loved to paint rugged scenes with mountains, waterfalls, and rivers. Indeed, the Chinese word for "landscape" means "mountain-water." The Chinese considered mountains sacred places where spirits lived. Vertical scrolls with mountain landscapes might reach as high as seven feet. Small round or square paintings were sometimes made to cover a fan or to be placed in albums. Artists also loved to make **panoramic** rolls, enormous paintings that were kept rolled up in a box. You would unroll the painting slowly, as if following the artist in a journey across the vast landscape or scene.

Hui Zong opened many painting schools and promoted art and artists within his court. The palace even had an artist on call all night long just in case the emperor wanted something painted in the middle of the night.

Artists in Song China became known for their landscape paintings.

Military Problems

Some officials in Hui Zong's palace thought he spent too much time with his paintings and not enough time worrying about China's military problems. Several foreign tribes had moved across the northern border and were fighting for control of northern China. Hui Zong made a deal with one of the tribes, the Jurchen (/jur*chen/), to fight on China's side. Hui Zong thought that he had solved the problem and went back to his paintings. But when the Jurchen defeated China's enemies, they turned against the Chinese.

Vocabulary

panoramic, adj. giving a wide view of an area

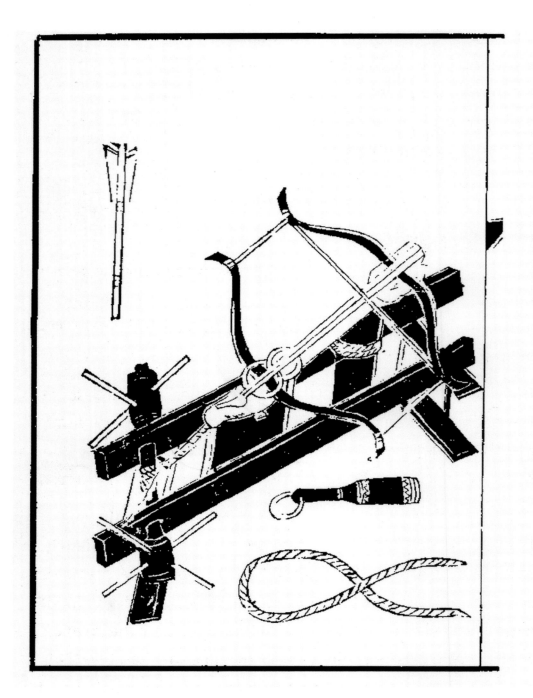

Chinese soldiers used crossbows to defend their capital city but were unable to stop the Jurchen from destroying it.

In 1126 the Jurchen attacked Hui Zong's capital at Kaifeng (/ky*fung/). Forty-eight thousand soldiers defended Kaifeng with crossbows and flamethrowers. But the Jurchen had even more powerful weapons. They brought in **siege machines** with movable towers that were so high they reached above the city walls. The attackers propelled firebombs over the walls into the city.

The "Duke of Confused Virtues"

The siege of Kaifeng lasted for more than a month. The Jurchen destroyed the city and captured Hui Zong. They took off his fine clothes and made him put on a servant's robes. Then the captors made fun of him by calling him the "Duke of Confused **Virtues**."

The Jurchen sent Hui Zong to the far northeast as their prisoner. The peddler's curse had come true. The emperor's power and wealth had vanished like smoke. He had no pride left. How Hui Zong yearned to see a simple Chinese pancake again! After nine hard years, Hui Zong died, still a prisoner of the Jurchen.

The Jurchen thought they had captured all of Hui Zong's family, but one of his sons escaped from them. He fled to the south, set up his own capital at Hangzhou (/hahng*joh/), and proclaimed himself emperor. He made a deal with the Jurchen: the invaders would control all of northern China, the area that had been the center of all the previous dynasties, while the Song would be left with the south. It was humiliating for the glorious Song dynasty, now known as the southern Song dynasty, but the new emperor had no choice.

Chapter 6
Town and Country

The Rice-Growing South The southern part of China, controlled by the Song dynasty, was very different from the northern part, controlled by the Jurchen. The south was hotter, wetter, and more humid. It was a perfect place for growing rice, which grows best in standing water.

The Big Question

What was the difference between life in the countryside and life in the city in southern China during the Song dynasty?

Southern China had the perfect climate for growing rice.

Peasants did all the work of planting and harvesting the rice. At dawn a drum sounded to call the workers to the fields. They did not have fancy equipment. Simple plows and hoes were all that they used. The plows were pulled by the men themselves or, if the men were lucky enough to have them, by water buffalo. The peasants labored hard in the fields, especially from June to September.

Rice became the most important part of the Chinese diet during the Song dynasty. The residents in the capital city of Hangzhou, a city numbering over one million people, ate about 220 **tons** of rice every single day. In Hangzhou you could buy many different kinds of rice. Some of the varieties included white rice, rice with lotus-pink grains, yellow-eared rice, rice on the stalk, pink rice, yellow rice, and old rice. All these different kinds of rice had to be grown and harvested. It's no wonder the poor peasants had to work so hard!

> **Vocabulary**
>
> **ton,** n. a unit of weight equal to two thousand pounds

City Pleasures

Many peasants left their fields and villages and moved into the city. The city amazed them. Peasant life was difficult and offered few pleasures. Hangzhou, by contrast, throbbed with constant activity.

Entertainers performed on the street corners and in areas of the city called "pleasure grounds" that were set aside near the markets and bridges. Here, performers of all sorts captivated audiences.

Puppet shows were one form of entertainment available in the city of Hangzhou.

In the image you can see lively street Life in a Song city.

You could stop to watch puppet shows and shadow plays; listen to music and storytellers; delight in jugglers, acrobats, tightrope walkers, and animal acts; and gasp as strongmen lifted huge blocks of stone to the sound of a drum roll.

City Streets

In the marketplaces and fancy shops, you could buy anything you wanted—pet cats, crickets in cages, even false hair. All of Hangzhou echoed with the noise of street **vendors**. They beat on pieces of wood or metal or cried out to attract customers. Their **wares** included tea, toys, food, **horoscopes**, honeycombs, and sugarcane. Some vendors sold "mosquito smoke," a powder for getting rid of the mosquitoes that loved the humid air of Hangzhou.

Porters rushed through the streets carrying goods that hung from long poles balanced on their shoulders. Enclosed chairs were also suspended from poles, and wealthy women, dressed elegantly in silks and gold brocade, rode inside them.

People in Hangzhou loved to eat and drink. Teahouses, bars, and restaurants crowded the streets, and pleasure boats serving food floated on a lake in Hangzhou.

Vocabulary

vendor, n. a person who sells something, usually on the street; a peddler

wares, n. goods for sale

horoscope, n. a prediction about a person's future, usually based on when a person was born and such things as the alignment of stars and planets

porter, n. a person hired to carry or transport goods

City on the Water

Water was everywhere in Hangzhou. The city lay between a large artificial lake in the west and a river in the east; twenty or more canals crisscrossed the city. Northern China was very dry, and the people who lived there rarely took baths. But southern China could not have been more different. The inhabitants of Hangzhou loved to bathe. Government officials got a day off every ten days just so they could take a bath. As a result, the Chinese word for bath also meant a ten-day period of time. The rich had their own rooms for bathing, but ordinary people flocked to public bathhouses. There may have been as many as three thousand of them in the city. Though the Chinese did not have toothbrushes at that time, they did wipe their gums with a handkerchief after eating. And they were the first people in the world to use toilet paper.

The Scholars

Amid the crowds strolling on the bustling streets of Hangzhou were men wearing special caps with long "ears." Only scholars had the right to wear these caps, and the only way to become a scholar was to pass a very difficult series of exams given by the government. The exams tested students' knowledge of the teachings of Confucius, as well as other subjects. There was even a poetry exam. Generally, no more than four or five hundred students out of four hundred thousand would pass these exams, called *jinshi*.

Confucius was a teacher and a philosopher. He believed in the power of education and promoted what were called the Six Arts: archery, calligraphy, mathematics, music, chariot-driving, and ritual, or cultural traditions. However, Confucius believed how a person behaved was the most important thing of all.

The scholars were the most honored and respected people in China; they formed an **elite** group and had many privileges. Over the years more and more young men wanted to become scholars, and the demand for education increased. The Song emperors opened many new schools. However, most children, whether they lived

Vocabulary

ritual, n. an act or series of actions done in the same way in a certain situation, such as a religious ceremony

elite, adj. having more talent, wealth, power, or privilege than everyone else

in the countryside or in the city, did not go to school. Only the children of elite families were educated.

Flammable City

Hangzhou was a crowded city. Its houses, made of wood and bamboo, rose up to five stories high. They were built one right next to the other. Lamps and lanterns with live flames provided light, but if one was dropped, it could mean disaster. From time to time, fires swept through huge sections of the city. One time, a fire raged for four days and nights, destroying more than 58,000 houses and killing many people.

Despite the threat of fire, people of Hangzhou thought they were safe behind their walls. But far to the north, beyond the land of the Jurchen, fresh trouble was brewing. For twenty years a nomadic leader from the Mongolian steppe had been fighting with the other northern tribes to unite them all under his rule. By the year 1206 this powerful and ruthless warrior had succeeded. He was feared by all and was given the title Chinggis Khan (/chin*giss/ kahn/), which meant universal ruler. You may have seen his name also spelled Genghis Khan. He now looked south to China and saw a country that in one part, the north, was under the control of the Jurchen, and in the other part, the south, was under the Song. He decided to pounce on China.

Chapter 7
The Mongol Invasions

A Frightening Trip In the year 1207, Jurchen ambassadors from northern China traveled a long distance north to the land of the Mongols. The ambassadors came to announce to the Mongols and their leader, Chinggis Khan, the name of the new emperor of North China.

The Big Question

What made the Mongols such fearsome warriors?

The ambassadors must have been terrified. They had heard about the fierce Mongols. Chinggis Khan had boasted that nothing made him happier than killing his enemies, stealing their property, and riding their horses. The Mongols lived on the vast open grassland of Mongolia in tents called yurts. They raised cattle, sheep, and horses. They looked down on the northern Chinese farmers and city dwellers as being soft and weak.

Chinggis Khan lived in a tent decorated with rich fabrics and golden **plaques**. He sat on a throne made of the skins of pure white horses, animals considered sacred by the Mongols.

Vocabulary

plaque, n. a decorative tablet, usually made to celebrate an individual or an event

Chinggis Khan, also called Genghis Khan, was emperor of the Mongols.

When the ambassadors told Chinggis Khan about their new emperor, they hoped that he would offer respectful words and congratulations. Instead, he spat on the ground, jumped on his horse, and rode away. The ambassadors went home shocked at this terrible sign of disrespect. Worse was to come, however. Chinggis Khan was planning a war against the Jurchen.

The world had never seen warriors as fearsome as the Mongols. Their children learned how to ride a horse before they could even walk. Then they were taught to shoot with a bow and arrow. The Mongols designed a powerful bow that could shoot arrows hundreds of feet.

Mongols learned at a young age how to shoot a bow and arrow while on horseback.

Because the Mongols rode so well, they could shoot an arrow with great accuracy while galloping at top speed.

The Mongols trained themselves to endure great hardships. They could go without food for a long time. If they ran out of water, they did not panic. Instead, they would just make a small cut in their horse's leg and drink its blood.

The sight of the Mongol attackers must have been terrifying. One historian living in this time period wrote that the Mongols appeared "more numerous than ants or **locusts**." And now they were headed toward China.

Terror from the North

The northern Chinese under the Jurchen thought they were safe because their towns had walls around them. But they were wrong. The Mongols thought up a cruel plan. They rounded up farmers and anybody else they caught outside the walls of a town. They forced these captives to march in front of the army, so when the defenders fired at the Mongols, they'd hit their own people first.

The Mongols destroyed ninety cities in northern China, including what is now Beijing. A foreign ambassador saw the terrible destruction of the city. He reported that a huge pile of bones lay outside the walls of the city. Almost every single person was killed, sixty thousand all told, and every building was burned to the ground. The ruins of the city burned for more than a month.

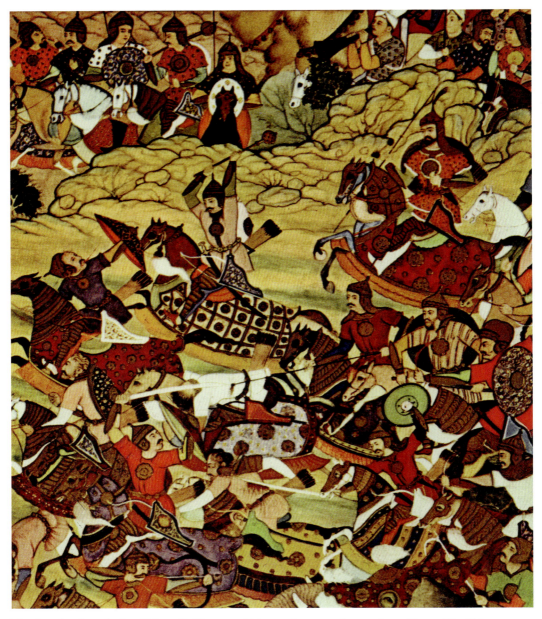

The battles fought by Chinggis Khan and his armies were legendary. Many, like this one, are still shown by illustrators today.

It took the Mongols about twenty years to defeat the Jurchen and conquer all of northern China. Chinggis Khan did not live to see the end of this war. He died in 1227. The Mongols did not want anyone to know that he had died. They took his body to a secret place and buried him with a huge treasure. A thousand horsemen rode over the grave site repeatedly to wipe out any trace of the digging. People have looked and looked, but to this day no one has found the tomb of Chinggis Khan.

The sons and grandsons of Chinggis Khan spread terror throughout Asia and Europe. They created an enormous land-based empire. It stretched all the way from the Pacific Ocean to eastern Europe. For more than one hundred years, a group of Mongols, called the Golden Horde, ruled Russia. The Mongol conquest of Russia was ruthless. In one town a monk wrote, "No eye remained open to weep for the dead."

The Song Dynasty Falls

It had been Chinggis Khan's dream to conquer all of China; his grandson Kublai Khan (/koo*blah/kahn/) set out to realize that dream. He unleashed his powerful army against the southern Song dynasty and its people.

The Mongols ran into all sorts of problems in southern China. First of all, it was just too hot for them. The northern men, as well as their horses, were used to colder weather, and they found it difficult to fight in the heat and humidity. Mosquitoes bit them, spreading disease to which the Mongols had no resistance. Many of the Mongol warriors got sick.

The Song had a strong navy and amazing weapons, such as flamethrowers, rockets, and catapults that could hurl bombs. Still, the Mongols proved what determined warriors they were.

Chinese Empire of the Mongols

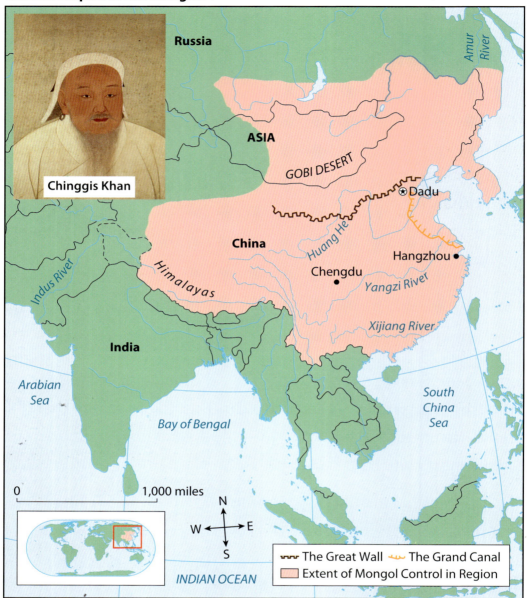

This map shows the area of the Empire of the Great Khan in and around what is now China, at its height in the late 1200s. After Chinggis Khan died, his children divided the Mongol Empire into four parts, and this was the largest one.

They built a navy of their own and developed artillery that could fire enormous hundred-pound rocks. The Mongols defeated one city after another, until they finally captured the capital city of Hangzhou and the five-year-old child emperor of the Song.

The mighty Kublai Khan had the young emperor brought to him. Everyone trembled at the thought of what the great emperor, or khan, might do to the helpless boy. The Mongols could be extremely cruel to their prisoners.

But Kublai Khan was not as cruel as his uncles and his grandfather. He had studied Chinese customs and admired many things about the Chinese. When the young emperor was brought before him, Kublai Khan took pity on him. He ordered that the child not be harmed and sent him away to live the quiet life of a Buddhist priest.

Chapter 8
Kublai Khan and Marco Polo

The Great Capital Once Kublai Khan conquered China, he decided to build a new capital city for himself. On the site of Beijing, he built a city and called it Dadu (/dah*doo/), or "great capital."

The Big Question

Why might the development of the postal service have been considered one of Kublai Khan's greatest achievements?

A bodyguard of twelve thousand horsemen protected the khan's family day and night. If any visitors thought they could attack the emperor, they got a surprise when they walked into the grand hall where he met the guests. There seemed to be tigers on a platform near the emperor. If you were brave enough to walk up to these tigers, you would see that they were actually mechanical models. The emperor had very clever inventors and builders working for him.

Some of the Mongols missed their old way of life and the grasslands of Mongolia. To make the Mongols happy, Kublai Khan ordered that huge yurts be put up in the gardens of the Imperial City. These new yurts were different from those their families and ancestors had lived in—they

Kublai Khan built a city on the site of what is now Beijing.

59

had magnificent furniture inside. Kublai Khan even sent men up north to collect grass from Mongolia. They planted the grass on an altar in the emperor's palace.

Kublai Khan was very interested in science. He built a tall building in the Imperial City as an **observatory**. He also invited a famous **astronomer** from Persia to Dadu. The astronomer brought instruments for observing the sun, moon, stars, and planets. He also brought a very special gift to Kublai Khan. For a long time, the astronomer had made careful observations of the movements of the **heavenly bodies**. He used these observations to calculate a new accurate calendar, which he gave to Kublai Khan. The Chinese called it the Calendar of Ten Thousand Years.

The Postal System

One of Kublai Khan's greatest achievements was the creation of the **postal system**. Kublai Khan wanted to keep tight control of the country, so he needed to be able to send and receive information quickly. He ordered that new roads and more than 1,400 postal stations be built throughout China. From one station to the next, horsemen galloped at top speed, carrying mail pouches. They had strands of bells wrapped around their bodies, so they made a loud noise as they sped down the roads. Other

Vocabulary

observatory, n. a building or room used to study the weather or astronomy

astronomer, n. a scientist who studies the stars, the planets, and other features of outer space

heavenly bodies, n. objects found in the sky, such as planets or stars

postal system, n. an organization, usually run by the government, responsible for sorting and delivering mail

travelers had to get out of their way. As the rider approached a postal stop, the men inside the station would hear the bells and quickly get a fresh horse ready. The mail carrier would then jump onto the new horse and head for the next station. On a good day a message might travel 250 miles. Fifty thousand horses were used in this postal system.

Marco Polo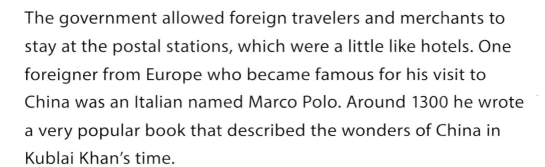

The government allowed foreign travelers and merchants to stay at the postal stations, which were a little like hotels. One foreigner from Europe who became famous for his visit to China was an Italian named Marco Polo. Around 1300 he wrote a very popular book that described the wonders of China in Kublai Khan's time.

Polo said that Kublai Khan's palace was "the greatest and most wonderful that ever was seen." He claimed it had four hundred rooms, with a dining hall where six thousand people could sit down for a banquet. Polo was amazed at the decorations. He wrote that gold and silver covered all the walls, along with gorgeous carvings of lions

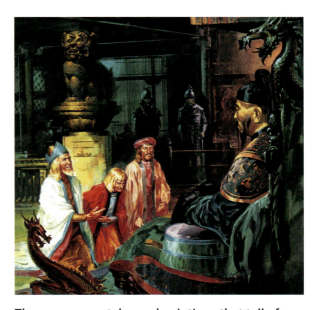

There are many tales and paintings that tell of Marco Polo's meeting with Kublai Khan. The truth is we do not really know for sure that Marco Polo met Kublai Khan though we do know Marco Polo spent many years in China.

and dragons. Paintings of war scenes also hung on the walls. Near the palace stood the khan's treasure houses, holding gold, silver, precious stones, and pearls.

Taxing Times

As time went on, the government needed more and more money. Kublai Khan hired foreign officials to think of new ways to **tax** the people. The Chinese hated these taxes. It made them especially angry to have foreigners in charge of the taxes. One of the foreign tax ministers was particularly evil. Some people believed Kublai Khan had been bewitched by this man's spells. Chinese officials working in the palace plotted against him. One night they lured him out of his house and killed him. But what would they tell Kublai Khan? Advisers convinced the khan that the tax minister had been stealing from him. Angry, Kublai Khan ordered the foreigner's body to be hung in the marketplace for all to see.

> **Vocabulary**
>
> **tax,** v. to require people to pay money or goods to support the workings of the government

Though the Chinese did not like it, Kublai Khan kept raising taxes anyway. He had to. He needed money to pay for his palace, his officials, and his luxurious way of life. He was also fighting wars in far-off places, and those wars cost a lot of money. In earlier times the Mongols had won almost every war, but now they were losing battles. They tried to conquer the Vietnamese people, who fought so bravely that the Mongols had to give up.

The Mongols also tried to invade Japan. Their invasion became one of the most famous events in all of history. Kublai Khan sent a huge fleet of ships to land on Japan.

A powerful typhoon suddenly started when the ships were at sea. The high winds and waves completely destroyed the Mongol fleet. The Japanese believed that the

typhoon had been sent on purpose by their gods to destroy the Mongols and save Japan. They called the typhoon *kamikaze* (/kah*mih*kah*zee/), "the divine wind," because they thought it came from heaven.

These defeats made the Chinese realize that the Mongols were not unbeatable. Some Chinese took up arms and revolted against Kublai Khan. When Kublai Khan's army put down these revolts, the Chinese people grew even more resentful.

A Famous Name

As he grew older, Kublai Khan grew very sad. His wife died, and then his favorite son, who was next in line to become emperor, died as well. Kublai Khan became ill. Still, he did not die until he was eighty years old. Like his grandfather, Chinggis Khan, Kublai Khan was buried in a secret place. Even today, no one knows where Kublai Khan is buried.

Chapter 9
The Forbidden City

The Not-So-Handsome Emperor
There is probably only one man in
all of Chinese history who is famous
for *not* being especially handsome.

The Big Question

How did the Manchu
gain control of China?

His name was Zhu Yuanzhang (/joo/yoo*ahn*jahng/),
and he was born in the year 1328. After he reached
adulthood, many artists painted portraits of him.

He had a pockmarked face and a large jaw that stuck out. But the
little boy with the large jaw grew up to become emperor of China.

Zhu Yuanzhang came from a very poor family of farmers. His parents
owed money to their landlords and had to move a lot when they
could not pay the rent. Zhu Yuanzhang never knew a real home.

When Zhu Yuanzhang was a teenager, the Huang He changed its
course and overflowed. Waters flooded all the fields and destroyed
the crops. People starved to death. Disease broke out and killed many
others. Both of Zhu Yuanzhang's parents died. At sixteen years of age,
Zhu Yuanzhang was an orphan. Desperate, he went to a Buddhist
monastery to ask for food and a place to live. But the monks there
were very poor themselves. The monks had no choice but to send
Zhu Yuanzhang, and people like him, out to beg for food and money.

Zhu Yuanzhang founded the Ming dynasty, which lasted for more than 250 years.

The Huang He, or Yellow River, is sometimes called "China's Sorrow" because of the destruction it causes when it floods. Zhu Yuanzhang became an orphan when the river flooded in the 1300s.

The Rebel

For years, Zhu Yuanzhang traveled around the country begging. He saw scenes of terrible poverty and suffering. People blamed the Mongol government for their troubles. The poor got so angry that they formed bands of rebel fighters. They stole food and attacked government troops.

Zhu Yuanzhang joined a rebel group and eventually became one of its leaders. When the commander of the rebels died, Zhu Yuanzhang became the new commander. In 1368, Zhu Yuanzhang sent a huge army to attack the Mongol emperor. The Mongol emperor fled back to Mongolia, and Zhu Yuanzhang proclaimed the beginning of a new dynasty, the Ming, which meant brightness.

Zhu Yuanzhang knew that he had a bad temper and that he could sometimes be cruel. He gave an order saying that he would let people write letters telling him what they did not like about the government. Zhu Yuanzhang promised not to get mad. But when he read some of the letters, he forgot his promise. One letter made him so angry that he ordered the author to be brought to the palace in chains and thrown into prison.

Because he had been poor himself, the emperor made laws to protect poor farmers from rich and powerful nobles. Zhu Yuanzhang made it a crime to take land from poor people. If you did, the emperor would have your nose cut off.

Zhu Yuanzhang ruled for thirty years. He made China a strong nation again. When one of Zhu Yuanzhang's sons, Zhu Di (/joo/di), became emperor, he decided that China needed a magnificent capital to display its great wealth and power. He ordered that the old buildings that Kublai Khan had put up be torn down. In their place he ordered a new Imperial City to be built. At the center of the Imperial City, Zhu Di wanted a splendid residence

Ming emperor Zhu Di built the Forbidden City as a residence for himself and his family.

for himself and the imperial family. The emperor gave this residence a frightening name: The Forbidden City.

The Forbidden City

Amazingly, the Forbidden City survives today. You can stand in places where the emperors' officials made their reports and imagine how they looked and felt. If officials had bad news to give the emperor, they trembled. Before they could speak to the emperor, officials had to **kowtow**, which means they had to kneel down nine times and touch their forehead to the floor each time. It showed that they had complete respect for the emperor.

Vocabulary

kowtow, v. in Chinese culture, to kneel and touch your forehead to the ground nine times as a sign of respect

The Forbidden City is surrounded by waterways.

The Admiral of the Western Seas

Zhu Di wanted to find out about other countries. He called for one of his most trusted soldiers, Zheng He (/jung/huh/), and named him Admiral of the Western Seas. He told Zheng He to build a fleet of ships to explore the world. The fleet included more than three hundred ships and a crew of almost 28,000 men. It was like a floating city.

The Chinese had invented the compass many centuries earlier, so they were able to navigate great distances on the open sea. On one voyage, Zheng He went all the way to the eastern coast of Africa. The rulers of eastern Africa heard that Zhu Di was fascinated by exotic animals, so they gave Zheng gifts of animals for the emperor. Zheng He returned with lions, leopards, camels, zebras, rhinoceroses, and giraffes. The emperor's officials were so amazed when they saw the giraffe that they bowed down before it.

Eventually, officials persuaded the new emperor that the voyages cost too much money. To make sure that others did not go on expensive journeys,

Explorer Zheng He brought back from Africa animals, such as giraffes, as gifts for the Ming emperor.

the officials took Zheng He's **log books**, or detailed records of his travels, and destroyed them. Nevertheless, Zheng He became famous for his voyages. He is considered one of the greatest explorers in history.

An Era of Hard Times

The other Ming emperors did not accomplish as much as Zhu Yuanzhang and Zhu Di. But they excelled at spending money, often on foolish things. The Ming emperors refused to save money by cutting back on luxuries. This was all the more problematic as many people were going hungry and poverty was increasing.

The situation got much worse in the 1620s, when the climate changed. The weather got colder for a while. Lakes that never had ice before suddenly froze solid. The summer growing season shrank. People starved. Rebellions broke out. One group of rebels broke the walls holding back the Huang He. Floods then killed hundreds of thousands of people.

The Coming of the Manchu

Eventually, a large rebellion broke out in northern China. The Ming dynasty first fell into the hands of Chinese rebels who captured Beijing. Then, incredibly, a Ming general opened the gates of the Great Wall and invited the Manchu to invade China. Over a number of years, the Manchu conquered China. The Manchu set up a new dynasty called the Qing (/ching/) dynasty.

The Manchu turned out to be very strict rulers. They made it illegal for any Chinese person to own any weapon. They insisted that all the Chinese be loyal to them. They thought of a way for all Chinese men to

prove their loyalty. For a long time, it had been fashionable for Manchu men to braid their hair in a **queue**. Chinese men, however, did not like that style. The Manchu emperor issued an order: in ten days all Chinese men had to start growing a queue. If a man did not grow one, that meant he was disloyal to the new government and he would be killed. Being forced to wear queues made the Chinese furious. They felt that they had lost control of their own lives.

The Manchu took over China and established the Qing dynasty.

Chapter 10
The Last Dynasty

The Emperor Who Possessed All Things The Qing dynasty began in 1644 and lasted all the way to 1912. During much of this time, China enjoyed peace and **prosperity**. The Manchu encouraged learning but also supported farmers.

The Big Question

What brought about an end to two thousand years of rule by emperors in China?

One of the finest Chinese emperors was Qianlong (/chee*yen*loong/). Even as a child, Qianlong showed great talent. His family gave him a strict education because they knew

Vocabulary

prosperity, n. success or wealth

that, one day, he would have great responsibility. He had to start his lessons at five o'clock in the morning and study until the sun went down. He had breaks to practice archery and horse riding.

The habits that Qianlong formed in childhood helped when he became emperor at the age of twenty-four. He rose early every morning and finished a lot of government business before breakfast, which he ate at seven o'clock. He had free time in the afternoon for the activities he really loved. He enjoyed painting pictures and writing poetry. In his lifetime he wrote more than 42,000 poems. He also

Qianlong was the fourth emperor of the Qing dynasty.

loved walking in his gardens. He had a beautiful garden, called the Paradise of Countless Trees, where delicate willows bent over fish ponds and fruit trees flourished.

In Qianlong's time, China became very rich and powerful. European nations eagerly paid high prices for China's silk, **porcelain**, tea, artworks, and other objects. The Chinese would not accept foreign money. They demanded to be paid in silver.

Vocabulary

porcelain, n. a type of fine pottery

China was willing to sell its products to the Europeans, but it was not yet interested in buying European products in return. Many Chinese believed that China made the best of everything and did not need anything that Westerners produced. Only a few Europeans were allowed to enter China—and only then during certain times of the year. The emperor made it illegal to teach the Chinese language to foreigners or to send Chinese books outside the country.

Qing porcelain, such as this vase, was in high demand in Europe, but the Europeans had very little that China wanted in return.

Great Britain became the biggest customer for China's

tea and porcelain. It annoyed the British that the Chinese were unwilling to buy their goods, especially when the British were spending so much money in China. In 1793 a British ambassador named Lord Macartney traveled to China with eighty-four assistants and advisers to meet with the emperor. They brought six hundred crates of British goods to show the emperor what marvelous products they made.

Qianlong received Lord Macartney politely. He invited the Englishman to a great banquet and took him on a tour of the private imperial garden. But whenever Macartney tried to discuss business, Qianlong changed the subject.

Finally, the Chinese hinted to the British that it was time to leave. The British told Qianlong's officials that they had not yet completed their business. The officials handed over a letter from the emperor. The emperor wrote, "We possess all things. I set no value on objects strange or **ingenious**, and have no use for your country's manufactures."

> **Vocabulary**
>
> **ingenious,** adj.
> clever

The British were stunned, but they could not argue with the emperor of China. They had to leave.

The Opium Wars

China thought it could remain isolated from Europe and the Western world. But the world was changing. The nations of Europe were growing richer and more powerful. They wanted to have influence over China, and they wanted to sell their goods there. China would not remain isolated for long.

The British eventually began selling a few goods to the Chinese, including a drug called opium from India. Opium is a very powerful and very addictive painkiller. Becoming addicted is exactly what happened to many people in China. One Chinese official wrote that opium was "worse than an invasion of wild beasts." It destroyed Chinese lives and families.

The Chinese government tried to stop the drug trade, but the British became angry. They were making too much money from opium. They refused to stop selling it. The British sent warships to force the Chinese to buy opium and other goods. This led to a series of bitter defeats for the Chinese. Whether they wanted to or not, the Chinese now had to open their doors to foreign traders.

In 1860, British and French soldiers burned the emperor's summer palace to the ground and stole many of its treasures: precious furniture, jewels, porcelain, and silk robes.

The British sent warships to China.

The Empty Throne

The great days of the Chinese empire were gone. Life became more difficult in China in the 1800s. The population got so big that the Chinese ran out of land for farming. There was not enough food to feed the growing population, and there were not enough jobs either. Many people left the country to find work in other parts of Asia, in South America, and in the United States.

Some Chinese settled in Hawaii to work the sugarcane fields. When gold was discovered in California in 1848, thousands of Chinese men sailed to the United States to work in the mines. They also helped build railroads in the American West.

China's ancient way of government barely lasted into the 1900s. A series of rebellions changed the country forever. Finally, in 1912 the last emperor of China stepped down from the throne. China became a **republic** with an elected government. After more than two thousand years of rule by emperors, the Chinese throne was empty.

> **Vocabulary**
>
> **republic,** n. a kind of government in which people elect representatives to rule for them

Glossary

A

academy, n. a distinguished place where scholars go to study **(38)**

alchemist, n. a person who tries to turn other metals into gold **(34)**

astronomer, n. a scientist who studies the stars, the planets, and other features of outer space **(60)**

B

barbarian, n. a violent or uncivilized person **(9)**

Buddha, n. the name given to Siddhartha Gautama, the founder of Buddhism **(28)**

Buddhist religion, n. also called Buddhism, a religion originating in India that is based on the teachings of Siddhartha Gautama **(22)**

C

calligraphy, n. artistic handwriting **(30)**

canvas, n. a strong, durable fabric made from natural fibers **(38)**

charcoal, n. black chunks of burned wood **(34)**

crossbow, n. a type of weapon that shoots arrows when the trigger is released **(4)**

E

elite, adj. having more talent, wealth, power, or privilege than everyone else **(48)**

emperor, n. the ruler of an empire **(2)**

F

foreigner, n. a person who comes from another country **(20)**

G

generation, n. a period of time of about twenty-five years **(11)**

H

heavenly bodies, n. objects found in the sky, such as planets or stars **(60)**

hemp, n. a type of plant, the fibers of which are used to make such things as rope, fabric, and paper **(19)**

horoscope, n. a prediction about a person's future, usually based on when a person was born and such things as the alignment of stars and planets **(46)**

I

immortality, n. unending life **(10)**

imperial, adj. relating to an emperor, empress or empire **(20)**

ingenious, adj. clever **(75)**

J

jade, n. a hard mineral, usually green, that can be made into jewelry or small figurines **(2)**

K

kowtow, v. in Chinese culture, to kneel and touch your forehead to the ground nine times as a sign of respect **(68)**

L

locust, n. a large grasshopper-like insect; in large swarms they can cause widespread crop damage **(53)**

log book, n. a journal to keep track of daily events, especially when traveling **(70)**

M

Ming dynasty, n. a period of Chinese rule from the late 1300s to the mid-1600s **(8)**

N

nitrate, n. a chemical; often used as fertilizer **(34)**

nun, n. a woman who lives a simple, religious life in a religious community of other women **(26)**

O

oasis, n. an area in the desert where there are water and plants (18)

observatory, n. a building or room used to study the weather or astronomy (60)

official, n. a person who carries out a government duty (15)

P

panoramic, adj. giving a wide view of an area (39)

peddler, n. a person who travels from one place to another selling goods (36)

plaque, n. a decorative tablet, usually made to celebrate an individual or an event (50)

porcelain, n. a type of fine pottery (74)

porter, n. a person hired to carry or transport goods (46)

postal system, n. an organization, usually run by the government, responsible for sorting and delivering mail (60)

prophecy, n. a prediction about the future (36)

prosperity, n. success or wealth (72)

Q

queue, n. a short braid of hair worn at the back of the neck (71)

R

republic, n. a kind of government in which people elect representatives to rule for them (77)

resign, v. to step down from or leave a job (27)

ritual, n. an act or series of actions done in the same way in a certain situation, such as a religious ceremony (48)

ruthless, adj. cruel; without mercy or pity (26)

S

saltpeter, n. a type of nitrate (34)

shrine, n. a place considered holy because it is associated with a religious person or saint (22)

siege machine, n. a type of weapon used to break, weaken, or destroy thick walls during a siege (41)

T

tax, v. to require people to pay money or goods to support the workings of the government (62)

terracotta, n. baked or hardened brownish-red clay (2)

ton, n. a unit of weight equal to two thousand pounds (44)

tribesmen, n. the people who belong to a tribe or a society (16)

typhoon, n. a windy storm with heavy rain; a hurricane (63)

tyrant, n. a leader who rules by cruel or unjust means (7)

V

vendor, n. a person who sells something, usually on the street; a peddler (46)

virtue, n. a high moral standard (41)

W

wares, n. goods for sale (46)

woodblock printing, n. a type of printing in which designs and patterns are carved into a woodblock and the woodblock is then dipped in paint or ink and stamped on paper or another surface (34)

Y

yak, n. an ox-like animal that lives in Asia (18)

CKHG™
Core Knowledge HISTORY AND GEOGRAPHY™

Series Editor-In-Chief

E.D. Hirsch, Jr.

Editorial Directors

Linda Bevilacqua and Rosie McCormick

Subject Matter Expert

Yongguang Hu, PhD, Department of History, James Madison University